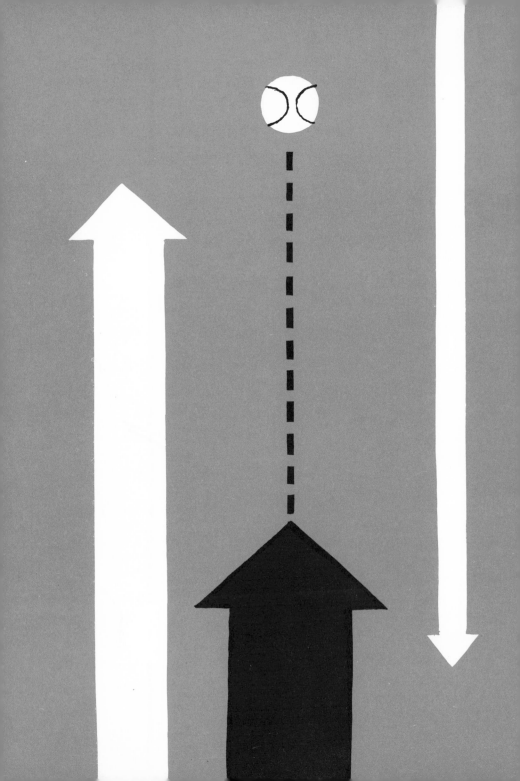

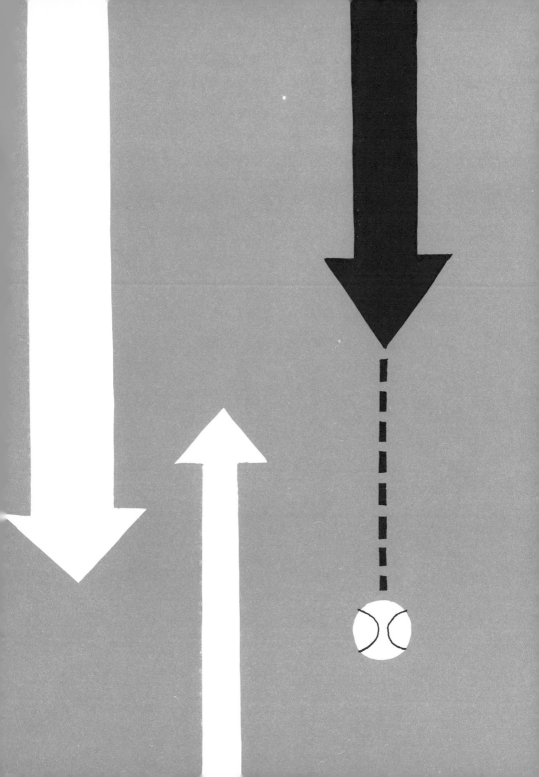

GRAVITY ALL AROUND

GRAVITY
ALL AROUND

TILLIE S. PINE
JOSEPH LEVINE

ILLUSTRATED BY
BERNICE MYERS

WHITTLESEY HOUSE • McGraw-Hill Book Company, Inc. • New York • Toronto • London

Also by Tillie S. Pine and Joseph Levine

AIR ALL AROUND

ELECTRICITY AND HOW WE USE IT

FRICTION ALL AROUND

LIGHT ALL AROUND

MAGNETS AND HOW TO USE THEM

SOUNDS ALL AROUND

WATER ALL AROUND

THE CHINESE KNEW

THE ESKIMOS KNEW

THE INDIANS KNEW

THE PILGRIMS KNEW

Published by Whittlesey House

A division of the McGraw-Hill Book Company, Inc.

As you read this book,
you will find out:
  What gravity is.
  What "up" and "down" mean.
  What weight means.
  What gravity does to falling things.
  How gravity makes our work hard.
  How we use gravity to help us.
  How we keep things from falling.
  How gravity helps you have fun in a swing.
  And—
you will even find out
how astronauts escape from the earth's gravity.

Jump up!
You come right down.
Have you ever wondered why?

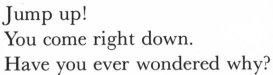

Throw a ball into the air!
It soon comes down.
Have you ever wondered why?

Lift your ruler up into the air!
Let it go! It drops to the floor.
Have you ever wondered why?

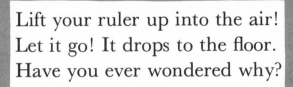

6

Something makes these things happen.

Do you know what it is?

It is the pull of the earth.

The earth pulls you, the ball, the ruler—
toward itself.

The earth pulls everything toward itself.

We call this pull—
GRAVITY

You cannot see gravity,
  but—
it is there!
  So—
when you
or your ball
or your ruler
comes down—
gravity makes it happen.

What do we mean when we use the words,
"up" and "down"?

When we say things go "up"—we mean that
they go *away* from the earth.

When we say things come "down"—we mean
that they come *toward* the earth.

WHAT DOES WEIGHT MEAN?

Step on a scale.
Read the number that tells you
how many pounds you weigh.
Do you weigh 72 pounds?
Do you weigh more?   Do you weigh less?
What does this really mean?
You know that gravity is pulling you
toward the center of the earth.
When the scale shows that you
weigh 72 pounds, it really means that
gravity is pulling you down
with a pull of 72 pounds.

Now—

weigh a book, a pair of skates, a shoe, a hat.
   Do all these things weigh the same?
   No, they do not. Why?
   Gravity pulls these things down.
   But—
the amount of the pull of gravity
is different on each of these things.
   So—
each of these things has a different weight.
   The more the pull of gravity on a thing—
the more the weight.
   The less the pull of gravity on a thing—
the less the weight.

What makes the pull of gravity
different on different things?

Do this.

Hold a dinner plate in one hand and a paper
plate of the same size in the other hand.

Which plate *feels* heavier?   The dinner
plate does.

Now weigh each of the plates on your scale.

Which weighs more?   The dinner plate does.

Why?

The material of which the dinner plate is
made makes the pull of gravity on it greater.

And—

the material of which the paper plate is made
makes the pull of gravity on it less.

So—

the dinner plate weighs more than the paper
plate, even though both are of the same size.

10

Now do this.

Weigh a large block of wood.

Weigh a small block of wood.

Which is heavier?   The large block is.

Both blocks are made of the same material.

But—

the larger the block, the more the pull
of gravity on it and the more the weight.

The smaller the block, the less the pull
of gravity on it and the less the weight.

So you see—

the pull of gravity is different
on different things,

because—

things are made of different materials
and—

things are made in different sizes.

Now, do you see
why different things have different weights?

WHAT DOES GRAVITY DO TO FALLING THINGS?

There is a story that three hundred years ago, a very famous scientist, Galileo, wanted to find out about gravity and falling things. He climbed to the top of the Leaning Tower of Pisa, in Italy. He dropped different things of different weights to the ground, at the same time.

What do you think he discovered?

You can do something simple to show you what Galileo learned.

Stand on a chair.
Hold a pencil and a shoe
high in the air.
Let go of both at the same time.

What do you see?
The falling pencil and shoe—
both hitting the floor
at the same time.

Now drop a marble and a ball,
a nail and a can opener, a book and an eraser,
a spoon and a slipper.

What do you see each time?
You see that when you drop large things and
small things together, from the same height,
they hit the floor at the same time.

13

You found out just what Galileo found out—
that gravity makes all things fall at the same
speed, from the same height.

But—
some things—feathers, sheets of paper,
pieces of cloth—fall more slowly
than other things.

Do you know why?

Air pushes up against all falling things. But
when light things fall, air keeps these things
from falling fast as gravity pulls them down.

Who knows this?

Parachute jumpers do.

They use open parachutes to bring them
down through the air, slowly and safely to the
earth.

What else does gravity do to falling things?

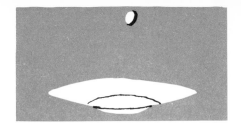

Do this.

Hold a penny about three inches above a plate.

Let it drop into the plate.

You hear a soft clink.

Now—

hold the penny up as high as you can reach.

Drop it into the plate again.

You hear a loud clink.

You found out that—

the shorter the drop of the penny, the softer the sound it makes when it hits; the longer the drop of the penny, the louder the sound it makes when it hits.

What makes this happen?

Gravity does.

The longer the drop of the falling thing, the faster and faster gravity makes it fall.

And—

the faster it falls, the harder it hits when it stops falling.

15

Who knows this?

Men who use piledrivers do.

They use machines to raise heavy, metal weights high into the air. They let the weights drop. The weights hit long, heavy logs or pipes and drive them deep down into the ground. These logs help to support different kinds of buildings.

What else does gravity do to falling things?

Do this.

Lean a long board against a chair.

Hold a ball halfway up the slanting board.

Let it roll down.

Mark the spot on the floor where the ball stops rolling.

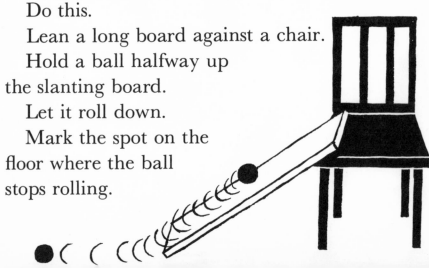

Now—
let the ball roll down from the top
of the slanting board.

Mark the spot where the ball stops
rolling this time.

What do you see?

You see that—
the higher the starting point
on the slanting board, the farther the ball rolls.

What makes this happen?

Gravity does.

The longer a thing travels downhill, the faster
gravity makes it go.

And—
the faster it moves, the farther out it goes.

Who knows this?

Ski jumpers do.

They start at the top of a long, steep ski-jump.
They travel downhill faster and faster, and they
jump ahead farther and farther.

WHEN DOES GRAVITY MAKE
WORK HARD FOR US?

Do you ever help lift furniture?

Do you help Mother carry groceries?

Do you climb many stairs in school?

When you do these things—
you work hard.   Why?

Put your empty book bag on the floor.
Lift it!
Do you have to work hard to lift the bag?
No, you do not.

Now put the bag on the floor and put three
books into it.

Lift the bag again.

You have to work a little harder this time
because—
the bag is heavier.

Put the bag down again
and *fill* it with books.

Lift!

You surely have to work
much harder to lift this heavy bag.

What makes your work harder
each time you lift the bag?

Gravity does!

The more the pull of gravity the more the
weight.

When you lift things, you work *against* the
pulling down of gravity.

So—

gravity makes work hard for us when we lift
things.

Who works hard lifting things?
Sanitation workers do—when
they lift cans of ashes to their trucks.
Plumbers do—when they lift
their heavy bags of tools.
Carpenters do—when they lift
heavy boards.
And—
you do when you lift your baby brother.

What do we use to help make
our work easier when we lift things?
  We use a crane to help us lift steel beams.

  We use a lever to help us lift heavy rocks.
  We use a jack to help us lift a car.
  We use pulleys to help us lift heavy crates.
  We use a ramp to help us get
heavy packages into trucks.

22

What do we use to help make our work easier
when we carry things?

We use a wheelbarrow to carry sand.

We use a truck to carry furniture.

We use a shopping cart to carry groceries.

We use a handcart to carry luggage.

What makes climbing hard?

Remember the time you went sleigh riding
down the snow-covered hill?

You surely had fun!

What helped you go down?

Gravity did!

But—

was it fun walking back up the hill?

No, it was not!

You became tired walking up the hill.

Why?

Gravity kept pulling you down
as you kept walking up.

So—

gravity makes work hard for us
when we climb.

Who works hard climbing?
Explorers do—when they climb mountains.
Firemen do—when they climb their ladders.
Acrobats do—when they climb their ropes.
And you do—
when you climb stairs.

What do we use to help make
our work easier when we climb?

We use ramps and stairs when we board ships
and airplanes.

We use ramps when we push bicycles and
baby carriages into buildings.

We use ramps when we store cars in garages.

We build winding roads up mountains.

These winding roads are really ramps.

How do ramps make our work easier?

They let us work more slowly against gravity
—a little bit at a time. This makes
climbing easier for us.

So you see—
gravity makes work hard for us
in many different ways.

HOW DO WE KEEP THINGS
FROM FALLING?

You know that gravity pulls
all things down.

But—

do you know how we can keep things
from falling?

You can do some simple things
to find out.

Tie a string to a ruler.

Hold the string so that the ruler
hangs freely.

What keeps the ruler from falling?

The string does.

We call this string a *support*.

Now—cut the string.

What happens?

The ruler falls to the floor.   Why?

You removed the support that holds
the ruler in the air.

And—

gravity pulls the ruler down.

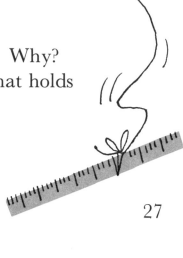

Now—
build a bridge of blocks or books.
 What keeps the bridge up?
 The "piers" do.
 We call the piers—supports.
 Pull out one pier.
 What happens?
 The bridge falls.   Why?
 You removed one support of the bridge.
 And—
gravity pulls the bridge down.
 Now you know that—
we can keep things from falling.
 We use supports of all kinds.

28

We build—
    piers for bridges,
    foundations and walls for houses.
We use—
    ropes to keep swings up,
    hooks to keep pictures on the walls,
    shelves to hold dishes and books,
    brackets to hold up lights.

We also use—
poles for flags and sails,
poles for lights and sirens,
poles for signs and antennas.

BUS
STOP

HOW DO WE USE GRAVITY
TO HELP US?

When you go outdoors, look at the street.
See how the road slants toward the curbs.
Next time it rains, watch how
the rain water flows toward the curbs
and down toward the sewer openings.
How does this happen?
Do this and you will understand.
Place a ball on a small table.
The ball stays where you put it
because—
the flat table keeps the ball from falling.
Gravity cannot make the ball roll
off the table.
Now—
raise one end of the table a little bit.
What do you see?
The ball starts to roll
and then—
falls to the floor. Why?
The slanted table cannot support the ball.
Gravity makes the ball roll and fall
off the table.

Now do this.

Pour a glass of water
on the drainboard of the sink.

Does the water stay on the drainboard?

No, it does not. Why?

The board is slanted.
It cannot support the water.

Gravity pulls it down.

Now you know why builders of streets make
the streets slant.

They use gravity to help them.

Gravity pulls the rain water
down the slanty roads toward the sewer openings.

In the same way—
rain water and melting snows
flow down mountain sides to streams.

Streams flow down to rivers.

Rivers flow down to the seas.

Water also flows down through pipes from
reservoirs and lakes high in the mountains to
our cities and towns.

How else do we use gravity to help us?

When the coal man delivers coal, he does not carry the coal.

He uses a chute. Gravity helps him.

When truck drivers deliver heavy packages, they do not carry the packages.

They use a slide. Gravity helps them.

And—

when you go to the playground,
you have fun sliding down
the slide. Gravity helps you.

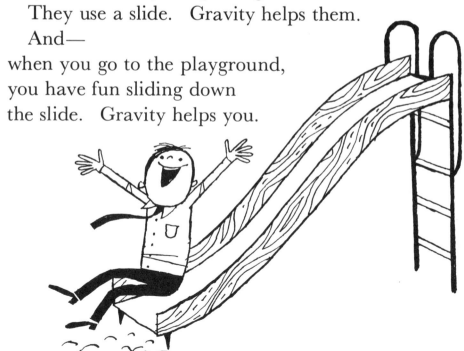

HOW DOES GRAVITY HELP YOU
TO HAVE FUN IN A SWING?

Remember the last time you rode
in a swing in the playground?
Do you know what makes you come back
after you swing out?
You can do something simple to show you.
Tie one end of a string
around a block of wood.
Fasten the other end of the string
to a table so that the block hangs freely.
Now—push the block a little bit.
What happens?   The block swings out,
and soon—
it swings back and forth, back and forth.

Why?

The block moves out and up
    and—
gravity pulls it down and back,
down and back.

    But—
the block soon stops swinging. Why?

The moving string keeps rubbing
against the place where it is attached
to the table.

The moving block keeps rubbing against the
air.

We call this rubbing—*friction.*

The friction on the string and the block soon
stops the block from swinging.

In the same way, your swing in the playground moves out and up.

Gravity pulls it down and back, down and back.

The swing soon would stop moving because of its rubbing, just as the block did.

But—
how do you keep swinging?

You push yourself as you sit in your swing,

or—

someone pushes you.

What keeps a pendulum in a clock swinging?

A pendulum in a clock swings back and forth, back and forth.

Rubbing, you know, would stop the pendulum, too, from moving.

But—

we do something to keep the pendulum swinging.

We put coiled springs into the clock.

We wind these springs.

As the springs slowly unwind,
they push the pendulum and keep it moving.

This helps the clock to keep correct time.

How is gravity helping in each picture?

Gravity helps us in many different ways.

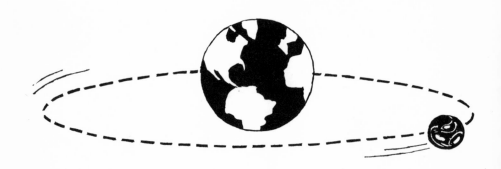

DOES GRAVITY PULL IN SPACE?

The moon keeps moving around and around the earth.

We call the moon's path around the earth— its *orbit*.

Have you ever wondered what holds the moon in its orbit and keeps it from flying off into space?

You can do something to help you understand.

Crush some newspapers into a paper bag.

Tie the bag with one end of a long string.

Hold the other end of the string.

Stand in a large open space outdoors.

Swing the bag in a circle over your head, around and around.

The circle is the bag's orbit around you.

What would happen if you let go of the string
as you swing the bag around?

Try it.

The bag flies off.   Why?

You no longer are holding the string.

As long as you hold the string
while you swing the bag, the bag will stay
in its orbit.

Now, suppose we pretend—
you are the earth,
the bag is the moon,
the string is the earth's "gravity-pull."

Then you will understand that—
the moon (the bag) stays in its orbit
around the earth (you)
because—
gravity (the string) keeps the moon
in its orbit.

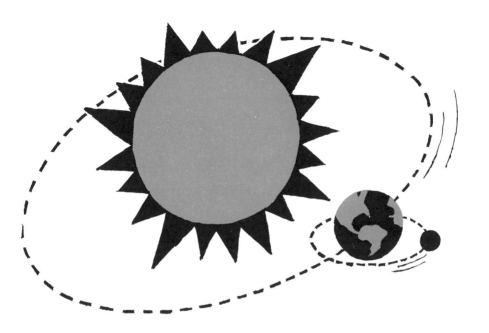

The earth keeps moving around and around
the sun.

We call the earth's path around the sun—
it's orbit.

Have you ever wondered what keeps the
earth in its orbit?

Just as the earth has a gravity-pull, the sun,
too, has its own gravity-pull.

And—

just as the earth's gravity keeps the moon
in its orbit, the sun's gravity
keeps the earth in its orbit.

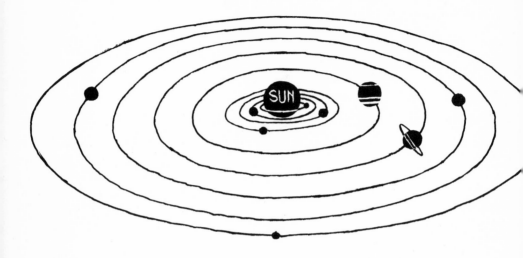

The other planets—Mercury, Venus, Mars, Jupiter, Saturn, Uranus, Neptune, Pluto—all keep moving around and around the sun.

Can you guess what keeps these planets in their own orbits around the sun?

The sun's gravity does!

So you see—

the sun,

the earth, and the other planets

all have their own gravity-pull in space.

HOW DO WE ESCAPE FROM THE EARTH?

When you throw a ball into the air,
what happens?

It always comes down.

No matter how hard you throw it, it will still
come down. Gravity pulls it down.

But—

can you believe that if you could throw
the ball up hard enough and fast enough,
it would escape from the earth

and—

fly off into space?

Of course, you cannot throw a ball so hard
and so fast. No one can.

But—

scientists *do* know how to send
space ships into space hard enough
and fast enough—so hard and so fast
that they can escape from the earth.

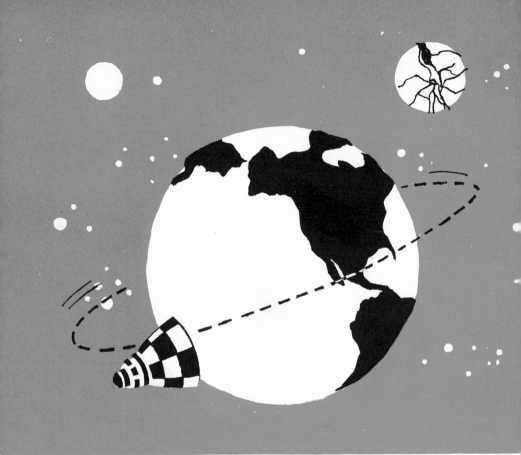

How do they do this?
They build rocket engines
strong enough to make a space ship
travel about eighteen thousand (18,000)
miles an hour. This is
more than twenty-five (25) times
as fast as the fastest airplane
you ever saw.

46

When the space ship travels *so* fast, it can
escape the pull-back of gravity.
    And—
we can send
    space ships to the moon,
    space ships to the sun,
    space ships to the other planets.
You found out many things about gravity.
    You know what gravity does.
    And—
you know—
how a spaceship can escape from the earth.

Now you will understand how Telstar can stay in orbit around the earth month after month—year after year; and how—
Telstar could bounce television programs from our country to countries across the ocean.

Can you believe that some day *you* may be a space traveler,
    and—
you may even visit our neighbors in space?

48

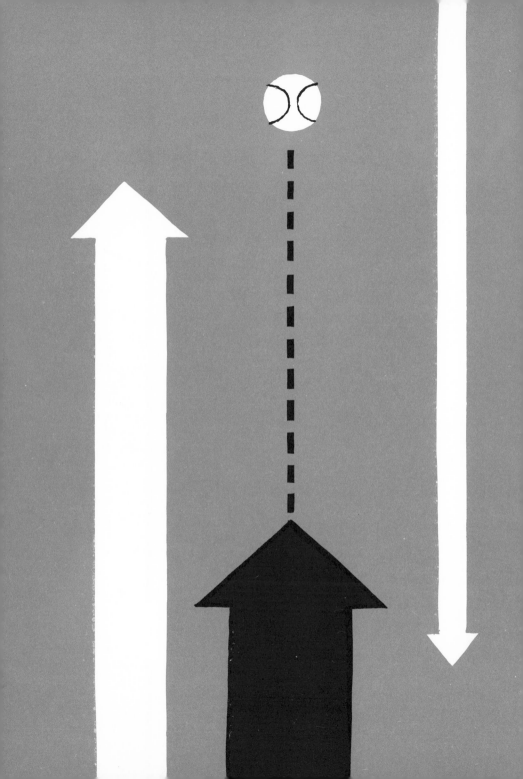

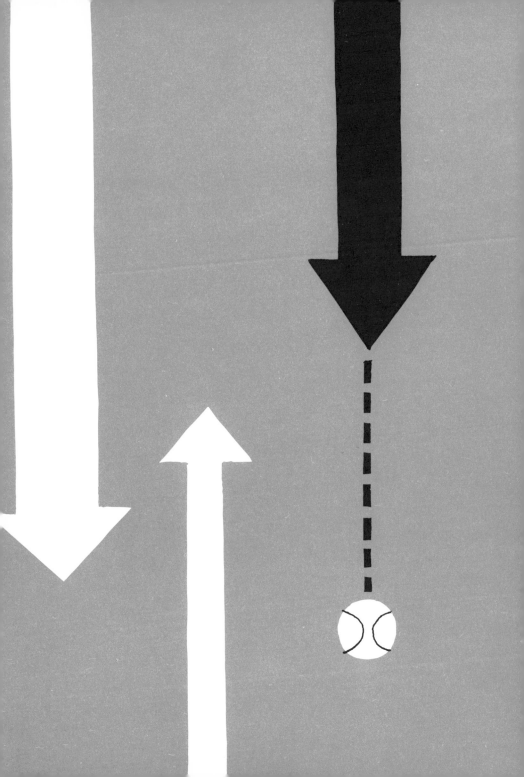